# Background Noises

### Poetry by

## Eunice Heath Tate

*Eunice Tate*

Akil
publications

Some of these poems were previously published in Reggae
Report Magazine, The Daily Gleaner, Ethnic Treasures and
Journal of Multicultural Heartspeak.


Special thanks to Denise Torres Robelo for her generosity
and for capturing the flavor of Background Noises. And my
friend, Joan Lane, for her invaluable help and support during
the process.
Nuff Respect.
*Eunice*

*Cover designed by Denise Torres Robelo*




Published by:
Akil Publications
P.O. Box 612574
North Miami
Florida 33261-2574

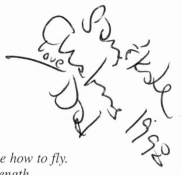

*To my children who taught me how to fly.*
*Shelley, you are my strength.*
*Dave, you were the one who taught me*
*to laugh at this thing called life.*
*Kevin, you are my inspiration.*
*Jamari, you are my sunshine.*
*You all are my heart.*

♥

*In loving memory of*
*B. Mark (Dave) Edward.*
*I will carry you in my heart forever.*

# CONTENTS

## *Pictures Of Jamaica*

| | |
|---|---|
| Background Noises | 7 |
| For "Daddy" My Grandfather | 10 |
| Don't Shed No Tears | 12 |
| Going Home | 13 |
| Life Hard | 14 |
| I Am Your Dream | 15 |
| Needs Speak | 17 |
| The House | 18 |
| Words | 20 |
| Love Child | 21 |

## *The Women*

| | |
|---|---|
| This Bitch | 23 |
| People Say | 26 |
| Mother Mother | 27 |
| Blues Song | 29 |
| When I See A Sister | 30 |
| Mama | 31 |
| If I Were A Poet | 33 |
| A Saying | 36 |
| This Is America | 38 |

## *Between Friends & Lovers*

| | |
|---|---|
| I Am Through | 42 |
| Insanity | 43 |
| Unlikely Lover | 44 |
| I Know Your Name | 45 |
| Conversation With Carl | 46 |
| You'll See | 47 |
| Between Friends | 48 |
| The Way He Prays | 49 |

# CONTENTS

I Am Woman 50

The Weight Of Silence 51

Not A Love Poem 52

The Cloverleaf 53

In Limbo 55

Valentine 57

## *Heartprints*

Who Am I 59

I Call You Friend 63

Speaking After Silence 64

The Loss 67

Missing Legacy 68

Poem For Our Children #1 70

Poem For Our Children #2 71

Poem For The Lost Children 72

Questions 73

Grown-Up Woman 74

The Untitled Years 75

Joy 77

A David Poem 78

Poem For My Little Sister, Donna 79

Reflections 80

# Pictures
## of
### Jamaica

## *Background Noises*

In a foreign land
I still hear the
background noises
of my homeland Jamaica
as close as a breath
their energies as
visible as the sun
sustaining my life
today and tomorrow

And I reflect on
the Ashanti family
fighting freedom's battle
Granny Nanny, Cudjoe
Accompong, Johnny
Cuffy, Quao
blowing the abeng
calling warriors to battle

And if I am real quiet
I can hear the feet
of the "Great Trek" marchers
over the high mountains
and wild forests
of the Cockpit Country

I can hear mothers
pulling back the skin of mangos
with righteous rage
gathering strength from their ovaries
to support their children
while fathers slip away
to lave in uncharted rivers

There noises are fathers allocating
a lifetime from a single paycheck
it's thighs crossed under
a breadfruit tree
awaiting the slow birth of trust

These sounds are
as simple as neighbors
knowing each others' names
they are friends
among strangers

It's taking time out
to say 'good morning
and how do you do'

It's a lifetime of
education given
over braiding hair

These noises
ringing in my ears are
people catching people
Hush
Listen

It's Mother Joe son
squeezing my honey
getting some of the
finest rhythm
the island as ever born

It's Beres Hammond's Sweetness
Bob Marley's Buffalo Soldier
Gregory Issacs's Night Nurse
Beenie Man's Slam

These noises are cultured
sometimes raw
always strong
pride-filled
beating with the
sounds of struggle

It's the dread
selling jerk chicken
at Sam Sharpe square

It's Brother Shortie's
finger licking ital
competing with mama's
rice and peas and chicken

It's the sweet sweet sound
of neeseberries
falling on zinc roofs

Haaa, these noises
breathe scars and feelings
as tight as the portraits of love
they leave behind

It's what I breathe
and hope my children
will weave into their lives

♥

## For "Daddy" My Grandfather

I have searched my memory
to see beyond
the blank stares of your eyes
long before death pushed
everything backward and forward
trampling on grudges like weeds.

I sat in that church
and listened while the preacher
told a different story,
going on and on about a life
of kindness/humility/unshakable faith.
I wish I could remember you in that way.
Perhaps you truly were like that:
loving children, life and God.
The sisters tribute spoke
of a giant among the men.

My eyes shouted to the congregation
why did I not know of all this!

Your daughter, my mother, told an altered tale
one trimmed with lawsuit and negligence.
Your sons scorned your passing
as if relieved from a burden
they had not the taste to carry

That day in church, I listened
to my mother humming forgiveness,
my aunt crying silently,
and in Sunderland we laid your body
in a tomb by the river
where on that very day my father
told me about the place I was born
and how my feet once dangled in the air
like the foolish poet I grew up to be.

♥

## *Don't Shed No Tears*

in jamaica
i survived
for a whole
lifetime
on cornmeal porridge
chanting like a saint
in miss campbell's church

so while bob marley
says "little darling
don't shed no tears"
i write so i can
turn my tears inside
my screams
vibrating walls

and i think about
a generous spirit called mama
wearing the faces of africa
who fashioned oceans
so i could step across

so bob, my tears
are a ritual feast
keeping four hearts
loved and safe
in my thunder

♥

## *Going Home*

It was at the crossroads one afternoon
my father pulled the fragile memory
from his blood, telling me of the small house,
a yard decorated with flowers
and the glow of sunset,
there he said I was born a Pisces
and emerged to meet the river.

I understand the embrace of rivers,
smooth, gray stones and bamboo trees,
hooting owls and chattering leaves,
I know the site of my soul's pulse,
the songs of the woods,
the callused feet of country,
simplicity ain't no stranger to my tongue.

On that afternoon when we left the fresh
and sometimes pungent smells of backwoods
behind, my roots circulated and settled in my
blood. I then knew home where the soul rests.

♥

## *Life Hard*

Every day dem a cry
life hard down a yard
no money nah run
life hard ina jam down

One time salt fish
wen de shingle house top
now it gone way up
rice married
even common onion
a play big ting these days

Every day life hard
life hard down a yard, but stop!
yu nuh see how sophisticated
dem higler dun de get
dem a sport big hundred dalla
american hair style
wha me an yu can't afford
jewelry nuh stop yah
and chile young bwoy
a rush dem like crazy
an a gal touch dem man
choa! a worries

'Cause a foreign money
a run tings down de
every body a pray
fah somethin fi happen
crying life hard down yah
life hard ina jam down

♥

## *I Am Your Dream*

I come from vibrant
coco-colored
conscious women
I come from strength

Arch movements
righteous rhythm
seeking fulfillment
sound reasoning
I come from some
bad exchange

I come from festering wounds
that have never been loved clean
I come from pain
I come from love

I come from cruelty, ignorance
being robbed, stripped, abused
I come from some deep fear

I come from kings, queens
chains, dungeons, hunger
tears, degradation
I come from needs

I come from laughter,
sorrows' kitchen
some fine bad mamas
I come from warriors
freedom bound
I come from courage

I come from the finest
black pride
I come from joy,
sun-drenched shores
I come from tropical breeze
palm trees, tall cool drinks
I come from beauty

Baby
I am
your
dream

♥

## *Needs Speak*

puss gone
rat tek charge
poetic justice
some woulda sey

cause nite upon nite
me lie down
ina dis a bed
waiting for what
pastor sey
is rightfully mine
me mouth touching de roof
waiting
while im a get it
like it a guh outta style

see yah
me a eat salt
suh wa me fi duh
me a fi tek it
weh me can get it

♥

## *The House*

She lives there still, the last time I went back. A tiny
thing now, not the giant she was when she seduced
me. Tucked away at the end of the quiet dirt road,
nestled between the river and the narrow dirt path.
The bushes now grow as tall as light poles.
Ripe mangos and June plums cover the roadside
like yellow green blooms attracting flies.
The fruit trees more fragrant than the memory.
The river down the steep hillside, now drifting
between sad gray stones. It is Saturday, Mama's
voice catches up with me down the fruit-lined road,
bare feet skipping to the sultry music
inside my head."Walk good and mecase come back!"

I have gone for years thinking about those days
of innocence, when I came fresh from the city,
and she breathed new life into me and made me
feel things in a way I didn't believe possible.
Those days were good days, when I would lay
inside of her thinking about what I was to become.
She now belongs to a petty merchant who breezes
through the countryside with obvious disdain.
Stripped of her glory by decades of neglect
and the hostility of relatives fighting
to have her. I have seen her bend to the east
catching the sun in blunt slits of old wounds.
Her white body a dirty bleached-blond, bleeding
from lack of care. The big oak tree I used to play

under now arched like an eyebrow,
casting more shadows
with each season. I have searched her face
for years in this one, old photograph
I have of her, trying to taste
the bliss of being blameless.
To romp on the long white veranda,
where the sun strikes first every morning,
to hear Mama's voice call out to me, "Be careful,
nuh stain yuh church dress." And from the room
where my parents loved with ease, my father's voice
came, not unlike the random noise in a radio receiver,
"Listen to yuh Madda, Sophie."

The family are all scattered now. Four sisters
that came to us in transit
one summer when their parents migrated
to England. Three sisters living in America.
Mama in another part of the world.
Papa living like a tourist
between the Caribbean and America.
But what I wouldn't give
to have her again. If only for a summer.
A long beautiful summer
with the merciless Caribbean sun
on our backs. And the river playing our song
down the long quiet dirt road.

♥

## *Words*

There are no words
in this poem
only breaths
and tongues
and eyes
and mouths
and legs
and arms
and breasts
and ovaries
and vaginas
and blood
and memories

No words
are necessary
we speak
the language
of exiles

♥

## *Love Child*

I was born
out of wedlock
I am not a
bastard
illegitimate
half-nothing
I am a daughter

Under a
Sunderland sunset
papa seeded with love
mama carried me with pride

I am a love child

♥

*The Women*

## *This Bitch*

this black bitch
nigger
whore
as you see fit
to call me
have been
feeding you
nursing you
educating you
sustaining you
with the very fabric
of the blackness
that you fear      loathe

this bitch
have been working
in kitchens
in nurseries
cleaning
dusting
nursing
carrying the residue
of your hatred for
hundreds of years

this bitch had lives
pushed into her when
her legs were locked
in protest
this bitch hid herself
in dark places
to love you

this bitch held you up
when you were weak
turned over clouds
with her bare hands
to raise your children

validated you
nurtured you
polished your scars
until you could
look in the mirror and smile

yes, she
proudly carry the stretch marks
of her ancestors
in the folds of her face
the maps in her palms
the plantations on her feet
the graves in her eyes

this bitch
as you see fit to call me
showed you places
you would not
otherwise have seen
without her strength
her support
her forgiveness

you see
she is your
mother
wife
girlfriend
teacher
housekeeper

nurse
aunt
cousin
the taste in your mouth

black
proud
swinging hips
high behind
she is
your desire
your dream
your crave

this bitch
as you see fit
to call me
is woman

♥

## *People Say*

that I am a
resilient woman
that I don't break
I only bend

my mama
was like that too
and her mama
before that
now there are
four generations
of women
trying to
straighten out
from all that bending

♥

## *Mother Mother*

from darkness
came the light
we call children

we talk the talk
we walk the walk
we dance the dance
loving in circles

we look at love
with candid eyes
in fields where
wisdom blossoms
with the seasons
our songs lusty veins

not a word slithered
from our tongues
unmeasured
unweighed
unaccounted for

we slip, slide,
bend, skip, stretch
to the beat of evolution
we rest to draw from the well
but we dare not fall

we are the music
strumming violins
sweet, sweet
slow jazz
we are the drums
beating with crapulent fury
blood and wine
we are the untoasted
movers and shakers

we are
the flow
the swell
lapping against time
the builders of lives
the givers of wings
we're confident
we're not conceited

wherever we're from
whatever we're called
we are mother
mama, ma
mom, mommy
woman

♥

## *Blues Song*

It is sad that women wear
domestic scars like a gown
spilling their guts
in ceremonial silence

It is sad how women
defend their wounds in the light
sleep-walking through
the steady flow of braided apologies
making unwilling pupils
of their daughters

It is sad that sisters see fit
to decorate their insides
with the heaviness of men
and in their frosty consenting cells
boast bloodshot eyes
instead of their crowns

Even sadder
are the children
that will salute
the insanity tomorrow
their dreams tormenting stars

Or, will they manage to
recover your flesh
from those breathless cycles
and drink heavenly breaths

♥

## *When I See A Sister*

when i see a sister crying
i want to write her a dream
that wipe-out bad lovers
abusive husbands
ungrateful children
not-to-be trusted friends

i want to say
there's no mountain too high
i want to remind her
better will come one day

i rush to say
God is not asleep
and Jah love guides

i want to say
a heart is only blood
and it regenerates itself
for the next sunrise

i want to scream
the politicians
who drain your veins
in their morning cups
will live to cough up rusted blood

and i want to say
a brothers
that inflict pain
can also heal

♥

## *Mama*

Mama
for years
I listened
to your smiles
to find
the source
of sadness
behind your face

You disguised
so well the occasional
gin before bedtime
I didn't know the hollow
in your bottom lip
was not a beauty mark

And I often wondered
why you chew on wind
like an hungry child
your breast sags
in muted defeat

Mama
the part of me
that screams your name
I proudly maintain

You see mama
in your finest
unstyled hour
you are
Nanny
Winnie
Sheba
Zora
Harriet
Sojourner

♥

## *If I Were A Poet*

If I were a poet,
I would say hey brother
yes, you! it's all right
and I would caress that pain that
you haven't yet given a name
and I would hold you
and love you
until you uncoil
and embrace those words
which are really nothing
but feelings spilling over

If I were a poet
I would find words, words
that would make a difference
to the teenage mother
without self-esteem
I would tell you it is okay
to stumble, even fall
but have the courage to
rise and stand tall
words that would start fires
burning away all the self-hatred and
pain to which you laid claim
words that would lead to deliverance

Yeah, soft words, strong words
brave words, crying words
I would leave trails to be followed
a passage that would take us
back to the mother-land
there would be no need for you
to recede into nothingness or self-hatred

If I were a poet
I would march right up
to the President
and I would say
forget the damn apology
recognize my rights now
don't throw me crumbs to get my vote
I'm not sub-human, minority nothing
allow me to feed my children with dignity
do not misinform, miseducate them
with a curriculum that bears
no resemblance to their history

And as for Black History month
why do we as a people
get to be black only
one month out of twelve
I don't need crumbs
I need my name, my land, my prestige
since you brought me here
against my will
I want the right to walk free

If only I were a poet
this one tiny black woman
shouting silently in the dark
would retreat into liquid words
to create a brand new us

Yet here I am
choking on this bile in my throat
resisting the urge
to regurgitate my anger
at the emasculation of our men

If I were a poet
I would find the words that taste just right
you know, the kind that simmer until
it hugs your chest, until you feel free
words so strong, beat so consistent
they knock you over
before you have a chance
to catch their meaning

If I were a poet
I would want to say
Mr. President, unless you
can give me back
my history, my name, yes my name
my gold, my land
your apology won't mean
a damn thing to me

Unless you can rewrite history
Unless you are willing to help
correct racial and social ills
unless you can pull my ancestors
from the pit of the slave ships
wash the feces from their wounds
your apology bears no weight Mr. President

If I were a poet I would say
you cannot fight all the battles
so choose the ones you will fight
and fight them well

If I were a poet
my words would be a prayer
to uplift my people

♥

## A  Saying

They say good things
come to those who wait
well I have been waiting
far too long

I play with words
like a seductive lover
eager
hungry
in waiting

My legs opened wide
welcome a blessing
this tired heart
stretches across oceans
spitting up blood on contact

It is not enough
that my roots are
sprawled across the earth
for all the world to see
and dabble in the meaning
of my existence

My kinfolks
kidnapped
sold for profits
survived
so I could celebrate

Yet I'm sitting here
it seems always
attending wounds
mending bones

I have been
broken
mended
smiling tears

Rendered invisible
waiting for good things
to happen
waiting
still waiting
gathering scraps
for the vacancy

♥

## *This Is America*

it is sunday
but this is america
and rice and peas
is not necessarily
a sunday custom to be kept
carrot juice is a thing of the past
traditions get lost between
meaningless words

but this is america
children talk bad
if them speak in dialect
the school system
is a guessing game
name brand high priority
beepers, cellulars
metal detectors
are all on the menu

but this is america
children divorce
their parents
Lawd
parents erase
their children
in the blink of an eye
to relieve stress
or to be accepted
turn around and
become celebrity

but this is america
and people wear fear
like a shield
for the unknown
and sometimes
cruelty becomes
a weapon against
the unfamiliar

but this is america
men rape women
and get off scot-free
if them dare to
protect themselves
against STD's
and guess what
you asked for it
if your skirt is "too" short

but like i said
this is america
so many he-roes
and she-roes
yet the people dance
in denial
the good must suffer
for the bad
and where one race
is welcome
the other is scorned

but this is america
black men are
endangered species
said to be
marked for prison
targeted for early death

but this is america
the land of the free
where the disassociation
of a people
is pronounced
the connective tissue
decomposed

like i said
but this is america
blessed america
the land of the free
the land of opportunity
and the people must
have the right
to choose
or not to choose

♥

# Between Friends & Lovers

## *I Am Through*

there,
I am through separating
the living from the dead
the authentic from the fraudulent
I no longer will walk through
concrete and steel trap doors
like a virgin with jurisdiction
over ugliness

I am finished with shrieking in the dark
flirting with the brown butcher knife
making up what to tell the authorities
about your sudden barbarous death

it's over, done with, forgotten, gone,
go to her, live out the rest of your
wretched life as a regretful man
no one deserves to be submerged in this abyss,
the pungent fumes of hate

♥

## *Insanity*

The day you left
I locked myself away
in the silences of things
my tears rolled down inside
shattering bones and marrows

There in my self-imposed tomb
my blues laughed in my face

The day you left
the sunset lost its taste
the wind hunched over
in silent grief

The day you left
I walked on the edge of insanity
and I was sure I would not
survive the fall

But I did
and coming back from that tomb
I laughed at that thing called life
that makes women
step off the edge of the earth

Knowing that whatever future fires
return me to this path
I will live to someday smile
at my close escape

♥

## *Unlikely Lover*

He bore not
passion's name
but in his presence
my soul delighted

♥

## *I Know Your Name*
*for L.L.*

I know your name
by heart
it's guava jelly
on hard dough bread
avocado and bulla

I know your footsteps
anywhere
it's the occasional love
walking late at night
in boxer shorts
bringing me
water and ecstasy

I know your laughter
it's a
continent
a consonant
a vowel
that stuck
to my teeth like
sweet potato pudding

I know you well
you're a disappearing act
the hole in my heart
the doctor said
would take time to heal

♥

## Conversation With Carl

So liquid
was our
conversation
I felt your
response
kiss my lips
and I returned
home fuller.

♥

## *You'll See*

When I wrap
my thighs around you
they will feel
as strong and cool
as Blue Mountains.
You'll see.

And when you take the plunge
I will arch like a feline.
You'll see.

And it's your voice
that will be chanting.

You'll see.

♥

## *Between Friends*

My heart is not a friend
it has betrayed me once too often
but like a moth
I desire the flame.

Please don't burn me.

♥

## *The Way He Prays*

he prays like somebody
who stumbled on God
in the dark by accident

and the way he makes love
he makes love like somebody
has a pistol to his head
ready to blow is brains out
if he fails to satisfy himself

♥

## I Am Woman

you heard me coming
chanting your name
you think you know me
this black, green and gold
steel magnolia woman
whose secret river
you have stumbled upon

who are you
unconscious man
to capsuled my life
into one night of need

to brush aside
my female pain
by amputating my tongue

i am woman
i know how
to live on nothing
i have loved without
murdering the air
I chewed on raw flames
and silent death

i am the one who
drank hope nightly
so you could have a place
to release your semen

♥

## The Weight Of Silence

All else have failed
and while I would come to you with words
I know my words are not golden
they break under the weight of rejection
so I shall be content to stay home
pull loneliness around me
and make love to silence

♥

## Not A Love Poem

People say
i'm sensible
so perhaps
i should not be
laying here
beside you
naked
smiling joy
your snores vibrating
my pillows
my breast rising
and falling
to the rhythm of
your heartbeats
knowing contentment
breathing goodbye

So while
this is not
a love poem
(it is drippings
from my heart)
i feel what i feel
knowing
you will
scatter
me all over america

♥

## *The Cloverleaf*

i often wonder
have you ever wondered
what happened
that time long ago
at the cloverleaf
where we parted friendship
in heated climate
without touching
without tears
without second glances
without a meeting place
sketched out for tomorrow

we merely hugged the memories
to our bosoms and pretended
nothing but our pride mattered
those sun-burnt teenage years
you and me together
what happened back then?

did you know i loved you then
when we breathed, danced, schemed,
determined not to be the ladies
our mamas wished us to be
we were something then

i see you now
face cracked like
a woman grown frigid
from malice
you my sister friend

i see you
in hiding
a wing beyond mending
no room for me
to turn around and call you friend

♥

## *In Limbo*

I have been here before
wearing the face of a lunatic
spitting fire and brimstone
in the faces of gods.

I admit I have been easily seduced
by sad events and the soft face of deceit.

Yet I feel no shame in telling you,
though I was clumsy and careless
with my love, giving you more than
you deserve, and ultimately killing you,
I wish you would come home.

Does it help to know my soul searches
for you when you're not with me?
Or that my eyes navigate the space
we once shared, finding walls, ash,
forgotten socks and underwear, hair
in the sink and badly damaged memories?

Does it matter that nights make
a mockery of the woman I was,
or that my body shrivels up without
the touch it has come to know?
And your smells so freshly ancient
swell oceans and rivers, flinging
silence around like a tornado?

Does it matter that I wish lovers
dead on moonlit nights?

I told you I loved you.
You told me you loved me.
What happened in-between
to induce this exaggerated silence?
Does it help to know I am waiting
in the place you left me hanging in limbo?

♥

## *Valentine*
*to L.L.*

I forgot
how crowded
these rooms were
where we stored
our remains
us, not knowing
where that flow
would take us

I forgot
to forget
those tremors
on unloving days
how your words
now stashed
away safely
in the attic
of my dreams
were once a device
to unlock
stubborn doors
how your saliva
liberated me
how your hands
became poets
on those nights

♥

*Heartprints*

## *Who Am I?*

*for my mother, Dell*
*who often wondered who I am*

I.

Who am I?
I was darkness before light,
light before darkness,
thoughts before words,
liquid before form,
pure, perfect,
nurtured by your essence
I was you.

Fear was not a friend.
I had no ego then.
I was innocence.
I did not carry the burden of guilt.

Inside you, I once danced to the
rhythm of your heartbeat.
Love my only partner.

For a lifetime I lived within you
intimate with your feelings.
I responded to your gestures.
I knew your touch.
I was familiar with your voice.
See, I begin where you begin
end where you end.
I have no beginning, no ending.

II.

Who am I?
I am your other self.
The one who
baptized you mother,
crowned you womanself,
rendered you warrior,
voted you teacher,
shaped you father,
elected you medicine woman.
I exist where you exist.
Because you exist.

You wonder who am I?
can't you see.
I am daughter of the soil,
rainwatcher, catcher of tears,
the branches that stretch
from womb to womanself.
I am called many names:
your daughter,
your otherself,
now sometimes your caretaker.

III.

This color I wear is my inheritance, mama,
that my ancestors gave to you as a gift.
Can't you see who I am?

Open your eyes.
Don't you see the spot marked red
where you buried the afterbirth?
Didn't you plant the navel string
under a breadfruit tree
so I could grow and flourish with the times?

I can still taste the nutmeg on my tongue.
Don't you remember all the newspaper
you used to stuff in my chest
so I wouldn't throw up from car sickness?

Didn't you wake me up
from nightmares
when in the deep blue/dark
your face was nothing but a loving blur?
But I felt your fingers and knew instant comfort.

I am the one, mama,
who blew bubbles to give you a name.
Who held your finger because my hands
were much too small to carry my blessings.

Look at me, mama.
Take the guard from your eyes.
Stop this perpetual denial,
soul lynching,
counterfeiting ignorance.

I carry all your beauty,
beauty of the old village
on the west coast far from the sea,
where children played
ring-around-the-roses
without having to question
the kindness of strangers.

I know the taste of your saliva,
I have strolled the rich soil of your womb
and I know the contents of your smile.

Yet,
you wonder who am I?
I say, I am the one that made
you mourn the sacrifice.
The one you choose to give life.
The one you love to call daughter.
who am I?
look in the mirror,
the answer is waiting.

♥

## *I Call You Friend*
*for my sister Pauline,*
*who possess the spirit of a dove*


Sister — you wear it so well
this epithet that navigates blood
as ancient as spirits

When we were growing up
in our native homeland
soft dirt between our toes
we played roundas and prepared feasts
you had cause to dub me mother
but back then the rivers were clean
clearly we could see the stones
and I called you little sister

We grew up
gave birth to children
and pain and sometimes tears
and we always played an active role
in each other's life

Even when we were on a collision course
like two old cars in need of a tune up
we always knew we would get back on track
now, years later, you fit me comfortably.

So this sentimental need I have
to shape you with words
that would crown you sister/friend
with lifetime guarantee
is nothing personal
it just makes sense
♥

## *Speaking After Silence*

on this day
snowflakes
bleed down
boulevards
and melt
under the
weight of
another
murdered son
and everyday
since
whenever
i examine
my heart
i always
find it
bleeding
shrunk
charred
or in hiding

the city
has eyes
saw it all
drank the
screams
when God
wasn't looking
left the blood
as testimony

i will not
become
an angry
woman
25-to-life
will never
annihilate
your life
flesh stolen
from my
bones

i am not
an angry
woman
i will drink
from the river
with sad
gray stones
and disguise
myself
as trees
but i will
not become
an angry
woman

i will
not hold
my knees
and rock myself
to madness
or reside
in the seductive
womb of the dead

i
am
not
an
angry
woman

♥

## *The Loss*

it is on reflex
that come each
march and july
i sit looking
through red curtains
an exile in emptiness
the dark pit of my womb
now home for a name
i pronounced son

♥

## *Missing Legacy*

*for my grandmother who died before*
*I was conceived, but whom I would have loved*


I searched mama's face
for icons of you grandma
desperate for remnants of that self
grandpa locked away for safekeeping
from his young bride
I looked in corners, behind faces,
in the bottom of ships
where they might have forgotten you
hunched over in asthmatic discomfort.

I knew you had to be somewhere
so I fed mouthfuls of guano to the family
to see if they would sprout roots
but they were not liberal with their offerings
so I punched holes in laughter
dug through old boxes, family albums
where they might have stashed you
believe me grandma,
I looked all over for my legacy.

I was certain even if you died
before I was born, like you did
you left me something of you
something beyond the wide nose
the full lips, the generous spirit and
the clamor of my mother's breath
to support life
to call clan.

Now, I must mourn this loss
when your back have never arched
to hold me to your breast
your palms never soothed my cheeks
or your love anointed my head.

But this I feel,
I have been robbed, cheated
having not heard the rhythm
of your footsteps slice the air
or the tempo of your breath
as you call my name
and what I wouldn't give
to be consumed by your passion
to be overwhelmed by your generosity
to feel the embrace of your love.

♥

## *Poem For The Lost children #1*

Give them this day oh Lord
their hearts to wear.
Let not Air Jordan
be their daily bread.

♥

## *Poem For Our Children #2*

Brother recruit the blood
of their brothers,
celebrate their victory
in the glow of ignorance.
oh Lord give us this day
our eyes to see.

♥

## *Poem For The lost children*

Our children are
expelled from laughter oh Lord,
in a democratic country of surplus.

♥

## Questions

*(for anthony and the*
*one who got off scot-free)*

did he call my name
did he ask for me by face
when you plunged your
anger into him
did you answer his cries
with yet another blow?

what were his last words
can you give them back to me
was it the thirty seventh stroke
that took his last breathe and
sent his twenty four years bleeding
down Rochester streets, or
was your tongue the final assassin?

he never had a chance
did he?
not a prayer
against you evil cowards
now what will you do
when you taste his blood in your mouth
will your life be a constant throwing up
tell me, did he call mama?

♥

## Grown-Up Woman
*For my daughter, Shelley*


You call me Mama.
I call you Shelley,
Sophia, sometimes daughter,
and that's how it's been with us
when we were raising each other.

Years later,
we are still raising each other
through our daily talks.
It wasn't easy seeing
the way men looked at you
eyes filled with desire,
wondering if they were going
to honor you or rob you
of your confident strides.

You said you didn't miss
the presence of a father.
You said I am Mama, Papa, the world.

I haven't told you enough
how I admired you,
the good parts and the not-so-great parts.
I hope you know how fiercely I love you.
How proud I am to call you my other self.
How thankful I am
that you embody such fine spirit.

Nuff respect to you
miss grownup daughter.

♥

## The Untitled Years

They dangled
from scrubbed ceilings
of first impressions
circling the luggage
dragged in from the storms
cold, hungry for the dance
finding little comfort
in ancient promises

She washed herself
invisible to men
whose eyes she searched
for evidence of self

Heated nights
under violent waves
teeth clenched tightly
against screams
that would betray defeat
his manliness
splattered across the air

For twenty five years
she laid with him
participating in the erosion
waste really
of human worth

♥

From some distant place
watching her faith wilt
knowing she is
not to be forgiven
for she is an accomplice
to this crime of squander

♥

## *Joy*
*For my son, Jamari*

My son
who would
have thought
I would be
sitting here
missing you
like crazy

I see those small arms
stretch tall
around my neck
giving large doses of love
I see your
crinkled-eye smile
around every bend
in my life
peeking out like sunlight
through all the cracks

And I know that
joy is
a well-loved boy

♥

## *A David Poem*

my son
my beautiful manchild
i write this poem
in the darkroom of
trials and errors and
wide open doors
and always        always
i'm bleeding with you

so the words
pained my darling
as i scrape my heart
to bring you closer
and i must renew
my spirit to
carry-on with the caring

but i am alone
somber in the
wilderness of things
while i honor your right
for room to err

my son
my beautiful manchild
this poem holds you
dearly, gently, freely
for love
just won't let us be

♥

## *Poem for my little sister, Donna*

I've tried to reach you
with tongue and
eyes and soul strokes,
but you kept looking away sister.
How do I tell you I love you?

Sometimes love wears a quiet face.

♥

## *Reflections*

The nondead speak
insisting I respond
leaving scraps
of words          thoughts
for me to follow
back to myself
hanging up at the
sound of the beep

But tonight is not
for the nondead
The night is for david

♥